Ana's Music

by Angela Báez • illustrated by Jennifer Naalchigar

Lucy Calkins and Michael Rae-Grant, Series Editors

LETTER-SOUND CORRESPONDENCES
m, t, a, n, s, ss, p, i, d, g, o, c, k, ck, r

HIGH-FREQUENCY WORDS
is, like, see, the, no

Ana's Music
Author: Angela Báez
Series Editors: Lucy Calkins and Michael Rae-Grant

Heinemann
145 Maplewood Avenue, Suite 300
Portsmouth, NH 03801
www.heinemann.com

Copyright © 2023 Heinemann and The Reading and Writing Project Network, LLC

All rights reserved, including but not limited to the right to reproduce this book, or portions thereof, in any form or by any means whatsoever, without written permission from the publisher. For information on permission for reproductions or subsidiary rights licensing, please contact Heinemann at permissions@heinemann.com. Heinemann's authors have devoted their entire careers to developing the unique content in their works, and their written expression is protected by copyright law. We respectfully ask that you do not adapt, reuse, or copy anything on third-party (whether for-profit or not-for-profit) lesson-sharing websites.
—Heinemann Publishers

"Dedicated to Teachers" is a trademark of Greenwood Publishing Group, LLC.

Cataloging-in-Publication data is on file with the Library of Congress.

ISBN-13: 978-0-325-13796-4

Design and Production: Dinardo Design LLC, Carole Berg, and Rebecca Anderson
Editors: Anna Cockerille and Jennifer McKenna
Illustrations: Jennifer Naalchigar
Photographs: p. 32 © Ukki Studio/Shutterstock; inside back cover (rag) © Dr. Pixel/Shutterstock; inside back cover (shovel) © Vadym Zaitsev/Shutterstock.
Manufacturing: Gerard Clancy

Printed in the United States of America on acid-free paper
2 3 4 5 6 7 8 9 10 MP 28 27 26 25 24 23 22
November 2022 Printing / PO# 34910

Contents

1. Rock Music 1
2. Pip and the Rat 13
3. Ana and the Trip 23

Rock Music

I see a rock,
and I toss it in the sack.

Pip sees a rock,
and I toss it in the sack.

I see a can and
a rag and a sock…
and no rocks.

Tam can see Pip
and Ana…

and Tam can see a rock!

Tam rams the rock.
Ram, ram, ram! Crack!

I toss the rocks in the sack.

The rocks play music.

It is rock music!

Pip and the Rat

Pip sits
in the window.

Pip can see a rat.

Pip pats at the window.

The rat is on the can.

Pip pats at the window.

The rat is on the rim.

The rat sees Pip! Ack!
The rat tip, tip, tips, and...

...the rat is IN the can!

The rat kicks the can.

Music in the can!

Ana and the Trip

I am Ana,
and I am on a trip.

A pack.

A map.

A snack.

A rag.

Gas.

"And music?" Dad asks.
I nod.

Sit, Pip!

Rrrr, rrrr, rrrr!

Rrrr, rrrr, rrrr!

I am on a trip!

Learn about...

RATS

What animal can chew through wood, concrete, and even metal? Did you guess a rat? If you did, you're right! Rats are incredible creatures. Some people think they're dirty, but actually rats like to keep clean. They lick their fur to clean it off, the same way cats do.

Many rats live in holes in the ground so they can stay safe from predators—animals like cats or owls that might eat them. Usually, rats only come out at night. That's because the darkness makes it easier for them to hide from predators. Rats can't see very well, so they use their whiskers to feel their way in the darkness. And guess what? When it's time to go to sleep after a long night, rats like to snuggle up in their holes, next to all their family members. It helps them keep warm. Isn't that sweet?

Some people are afraid of rats, but in fact, rats are way more afraid of people. Rats only live close to us because we throw away lots of food scraps that they like to eat. To a rat, a trash can is like a humongous feast!

Talk about...

Ask your reader some questions like...

- What happened in this book?
- What are some ways that Ana makes music in this book?
- Why did the rat fall into the trash can?
- In this book, Ana goes on a pretend trip. Do you like to play pretend? What do you like to pretend?